Organization

Declutter & Organize Your Home (in 7 days)

Cleaning, Decluttering & Organizing your Life!

Introduction

It took me many years to find a balance between tidy and organized and slightly OCD. I used to clean and tidy constantly and although my home looked organized, it was the only thing that was, because by the time I had finished cleaning I had no time left to be productive in other areas of my life.

I grew up with the influence of a mother who liked not a thing out of place, and it rubbed off on me, I would even miss out on spending time with my children because there was so much to do in the house.

As time passed, I realized that there was more to life than cleaning! I realized I could have it all, a tidy, well presented, organized home, and an organized life in which I was successful at work and spent time with my family, and now I really do have it all!

I developed this 7 day plan to help people who also want to have it all. It doesn't matter if you have barely touched your home in weeks or if you are like I used to be and need to organize and clean less. This book will teach you how to completely declutter and organize yourself and your home in 7 days.

We will also discuss the immense benefits of organizing your home and how it can promote healthy and happy living for you and your family.

the information is without contract or any type of guarantee assurance.

Table of Contents

Chapter 1

The Benefits of Decluttering Your Home & Life

There are so many reasons that advocate keeping a clean home and decluttering your house. I'm sure that you know quite a few of them. However, that doesn't stop us from piling on the clutter, does it? Every now and then, even I stop, look around my living room, and say, "What happened in here? When did I get so many things!"

Sometimes it can be difficult to stay motivated enough to keep your home in a state that even your mother in law would be proud of (white glove test and all). However, if you can muster up the motivation to keep the clutter at bay, it is a great first step to keeping a well-organized and clean home.

Here are some of my favorite benefits of decluttering. Hopefully you can remember some of these helpful tips and considerations when you drop your purse, keys, sunglasses, and water bottle on the nearest counter instead of putting them in their proper homes.

You'll have more time for yourself. One of the greatest benefits from decluttering your home (and keeping it decluttered) is the time that you gain in the process. It might seem like you spend more time putting things away but in the long run, you will save more time than if you had to look for items that you've lost or power clean your home after a much overdue time.

You'll have more money. A lot of the items that you consider clutter would be useful for someone else. When we keep these things (that we don't actually use), they just take up space in our garage, attics, basements, and junk drawers. Instead of letting it take up space, why not let it go? You can easily make some money from these items by selling then at garage sales.

You'll feel more at home. I know that when my house is filled with clutter (like when I first moved into our new home and when we have to unbox a number of things in order to find items that we've stored away), my mind feels as chaotic as the mess that we just created. Living in a clean home helps to also put your mind at ease.

Living in a clean home can help you feel like you have more control of your life because, well – you do. An organized home is an example of one way that you can organize your life. It is the first step in doing so. If you can keep your home organized, you can take those organizational skills and put them into use in other places of your life.

You will even feel more welcome to guests coming over – which can even save you money. Having friends come over instead of going out with them can save you a fortune.

You will have more energy. Living in a messy home can zap your energy. Some say that it is because the chi in your home (as in Chinese Feng Shui) is off. Some say that it is because more clutter means more bacteria, which can cause you to get sick more often. I believe in both of those reasons as well as the thought that a messy home = a messy mind. When my mind is cluttered with thoughts, I can't concentrate and if I spend too much time in that state of mind, I just shut down.

You will feel more productive. When my home is clean, it feels both motivating and empowering. When I feel empowered, I feel like I can do absolutely anything. Not only that, when your home office or study is clean, you won't have distractions when you are trying to work in there.

You will have more time to get busy in the bedroom. A messy bedroom isn't sexy. Sure, we don't always need a perfect environment to get intimate with our partners. However, it sure does help if you don't have piles of dirty clothes laying around in your room. A clean room is one that is more likely to breed romance.

Chapter 2

Your 7 Day Declutter Plan

There are different ways that you can declutter your home (I will go through that in the next chapter). For this chapter, I want to talk about the basic steps that you will take, no matter what system you choose. These are the basic rules that you will need to remember to either purge your home of clutter or maintain it.

Step One

Identify Your Clutter

Being able to spot a piece of clutter in your home may be fairly simple. That stack of magazine. That pile of junk over there. This piece of...whatever this is. Clutter is easy to spot. Unfortunately, it is a little more difficult to define and identify.

In order to talk about decluttering your home, we must first talk about the different types of clutter. Yes, there are different types! Knowing what they are can help you avoid them in the future. Once you identify them, you will know what to do with them: throw it in the trash, find a home for it, or find a new home for it elsewhere (like a donation center or a garage sale, for example). There are six main types of clutter which can be found below:

1. **Clutter without a home.** This type of clutter isn't necessarily "clutter". It can all be important, useful stuff. The only problems is that it doesn't have a dedicated storage space or home. Because of that, these things tend to pile up.

2. **Straight up trash.** Yep. It's not clutter if it really belongs in the trash can. Then it's just useless trash that has been piling up in your home.

3. **Aspirational Clutter.** This are items that you buy in order to appear more interesting to others. This could mean a coffee table book or knick-knacks. This type of clutter is directly related to...

4. **Sentimental Clutter.** These are the baby blankets, pictures, ticket stubs, travel souvenirs, etc. that you get from living your life to the fullest.

5. **Clearance Clutter.** This is the clutter that came from the clearance shelf or basket of your favorite local stores. A lot of us have a tendency of hoarding this type of clutter because we think "It was a great deal" or "I can't just pass something up that is this cheap."

6. **Stocking up on supplies.** This clutter is only clutter if it is disorganized and if it gets out of control. I am a believer in being prepared. However, being prepared doesn't mean that you have to give up a clean home. A little bit of organization and some moderation will help you keep this type of clutter under control.

Okay now look around your home. Do you see examples of these different types of clutter?

Step Two

Go Room by Room

Each of the seven days of your decluttering plan should focus on one wing/area of your home:

1. **Outdoors.** This includes the backyard, front yard (any side yards), and the garage.

2. **Bedrooms.** This includes the master bedroom, kids rooms, and guest rooms.

3. **Kitchen.** The special area gets a day all to itself since there are so many drawers and little objects to go through.

4. **Study/Home Office.** This is pretty self-explanatory.

5. **Living/Dining/Family room.** There is a lot of clutter that gets trapped in these areas because they are places where the entire family hangs out.

6. **Laundry & Bathrooms.** The types of clutter that you usually find here are the hoarding of supplies and trash. This means both extra bottles and containers of things as well as the bottles with only a drop of liquid left.

7. **Extra spaces.** We don't all have the same layout in our houses. If you have any other rooms (attic, basement, storage rooms, walk in closets in the hallway), this is the day for it.

Step Three

Timing is Everything

You don't have to do all seven days continuously. We can't all take a week off of work so that we can dedicate specific days to cleaning. Instead, try to declutter your home in seven Sundays (or whatever day you choose).

In addition to that, consider the fact that you may get emotional while you are going through your things. Don't overwhelm yourself. Work for an hour at a time, then take a fifteen minute break. Don't forget to eat. I also suggest playing some music and making this fun. It only becomes a chore if you make it into a chore.

Avoid distractions. On days where you need to declutter, focus only on that. Don't worry about dusting or vacuuming. That is for a different day (unless you have the extra time). Your main focus is to get rid of the clutter. Besides, after you get rid of the clutter, cleaning will be much easier anyway.

Step Four

Make Everyone Drink the Kool Aid!

My husband says this quote whenever people fall into a system or when a number of people are following a trend. He says that they are all "drinking the Kool Aid." I'm not sure where it comes from but I do know that you'll want everyone in your home to follow your system (i.e. "drink the Kool Aid").

I try to set up certain symptoms in our home but they don't always get followed or get picked up. Sometimes it depends on what the system is and what types of people you are dealing with. Some people are more left-brained (technically oriented, prone to systems and organizational structures, and concrete ideas), while others are more right-

8

brained (creative, free-flowing, artsy, abstract thinkers).

Someone who is left brained might be more apt to go with a system that you implement while someone who is right brained might need a bit of coaxing. One idea might be to have that right brained thinker help you develop a system. Perhaps you can have him or her create a storage solution. For example: get the kids to organize the toys they play with into piles of how often they play with them. The ones that are rarely played with throw away, donate or sell and have a day out with the money, the ones that get played with very often put in an easy to reach organized place like a toy box or shelves, and the ones played less often in a cupboard or somewhere out of sight where they can get them when they want to.

Kids are tough. You may need some helpin creating their system. If they keep putting their toys in the wrong bin (or not in a bin at all), have them go with you to the store and pick out bins that they like. In addition to that, ask them where they would like to put their things. Stuffed animals in the blue bin and blocks in the red one?

Step Five

Be Realistic

Being organized isn't about being so disciplined that a little mess with make you have a nervous breakdown. I grew up in a house that was incredibly organized. Everything had its place. If I put something out of place, I was scolded. Our rooms were spotless. My brother and I have both picked up aspects of this lifestyle because of our parents. However, we took those habits and went in two different directions.

My brother has a number of children; they also have a dog and two cats. As you can imagine, his house isn't as spotless as our parent's home was. Because of the tension in the home, the disorganization, and the clash of cultures, my brother recently had a string of anxiety attacks. Since then, his therapist has helped him cope with everything: the disorganization and the clash of cultures mainly.

I went in a different direction. I am organized – highly organized. Everything in my office has its place. Each of my drawers in my dresser holds certain items. My closet is color coordinated. However, I still remember growing up in my parents' home. I lived in the house that I could not touch. I was scolded for things that seemed trivial to me. I didn't understand.

These days, I know that there is a balance. An organized home is structured enough so that you can find what you're looking for in less than three minutes. However, it isn't so organized that the thought of having a mess would make you feel so at ease that there is tension in your home. Your home must feel like a home, not a museum.

Chapter 3

Different Cleaning Systems That Really Work

Try the "Box and Banish" method.

This method is one of my favorites for when I'm just tired of seeing things pile up and I want to get rid of as much as I can. As an example, I'll talk about my office. The method works like this. I'll go into my office with a big plastic tote and clear off all of the surfaces: desks, tops of my cabinets, etc. etc. Sometimes I need more than one box. If I'm working with two spaces (let's say that I'm cleaning both my office and my craft room), I'll take different colored totes in there and dump all of that clutter into the boxes.

I take those boxes and go to a different space all together then work on the three pile method: trash, donate, or put away.

Another example of this is when we moved into our new place. We pretty much had a clean slate. We brought in our furniture first, then brought in our boxes full of clutter (and useful things as well). I had a whole storage unit full of stuff that I had to go through. I bet you that half of my storage unit is sitting in a donation center right now.

There is a problem with this method though. If you get distracted and you aren't able to go through those boxes at that time, it's like you just moved your clutter to a different room. However, it does create instant results ("My desk looks so clean now!"). Even better though, is if you can't go through the box, forget about it, and realize that it's still sitting in your garage three weeks later. If you haven't used those items in three weeks, chances are that you don't really need them in the first place.

"The Purge"

Purging your home of clutter is really the first step in a big lifestyle shift. In order to stay clean, you need to start in a clean home. For this system take these steps.

- Go room by room, focusing on one target at a time. While there, work from one side of the room to the other.

- When going through closets and dressers, make sure to take all of the items out and be honest with yourself when asking yourself these questions:

    o What will you keep?
    o What will you trash?
    o What will you donate?

o What can you give to friends?
o What needs alterations or repairs?
o What can you sell at a garage sale?
o What is just out of place?
o What have you not worn in the last 6 months?

- Each of those categories should have its own box. I like to keep a cardboard box handy for donations, a garbage bag handy for trash, and extra plastic totes for items that need to get put away. I call that my "go-back bin" (for items that are out of place and just need to be put into their homes).

- These specific tips may sound like gimmicks but it can really help to change the feel of your new clean space as well as help motivate you to keep going:

  o Buy new hangers for your closet. Use uniform hangers all around. I suggest clear plastic hangers with swivel heads or white tubular hangers. You can buy them in bulk and they work well.
  o Measure your closet space, cabinet spaces, pantry, and other storage spots so that you can buy containers and storage solutions that fit perfectly.

- After you have purged each room, make sure to set up a system to help maintain your newly clutter-free home. You can find maintenance tips in Chapter Five.

- Create a mud room. We don't all have them in our homes. Some of us don't have the space (myself included). I did claim a little alcove by the front door. In that space I placed a shoe rack, a shelf with baskets (pocket dump areas, one for my husband and one for myself), a small trash can, and hooks for coats. In front of the shoe rack is a small outdoor mat to help catch dirt. Mud rooms are an incredible easy way to help clutter at bay.

"The 'My In-Laws Are Staying With Us'"

This is another word for the "one hour super clean/declutter" that you do for your home when you find out that your in laws are heading to your place from the airport. The system works like this:

- First thing's first: take the clutter from off of the bathroom counters and either place them in their home or into a basket to keep under the sink. Then spritz everything down and let it sit while you do some other things on the list. Just don't forget to go back and wipe everything down. Do the same with the kitchen.

- Do a clean sweep of the bedrooms and tables by using fresh linens. Strip the dirty linens, throw them in the wash, and replace them. Do the same with the wastebasket liners. Think of what hotel rooms look like. You want to see clean, smooth surfaces.

- Dusting is obnoxious but a necessary evil. Dust from one side of the room to the other. Use a dry microfiber cloth and work from top to bottom, dumping all of the extra dust onto the floor. Then you can vacuum up all the excess.

- Glass should gleam. This means windows, mirrors, stainless steel appliances, etc. If it is reflective, make sure it reflects.

- Declutter the rooms where you will hang out in first before hitting other rooms like your home office or the bedroom. You want to make sure that those "public" places are clean first. Scan the room to see what's out of place. Utilize drawers by placing scattered items in them. That means remotes, magazines, and the like.

"The 'I Work From Home'"

I aptly named this because cleaning is what distracts me from work when I work from my home office. Instead of doing work, I get distracted by the pile of dishes and the stack of laundry to do. In order to stay focused, I work for a one hour block and then find something to put away. It keeps me from sitting at a desk for too long.

You can utilize this in your own home, even if you don't work from home. The basis behind this system is that you clean up clutter just a little bit throughout the day in order to maintain a clutter-free home. In between big tasks or activities that you enjoy, you can put away that stack of magazines or recycle those empty soda bottles.

No one says that you have to spend hours at a time cleaning, doing small de-cluttering task throughout the day does wonders to help your home stay organized.

"The Digital Clean-Up"

We rarely think of having to clean up our digital spaces but these are often the spaces that get neglected the most. The digital clean-up system is as follows:

- Back up all of your electronic devices regularly. You don't even have to manually do this. It can often be done automatically. How handy is that?

- Keep your computer and media files backed up on an external hard drive and keep them at least 30 feet away from your computer. This may seem silly but it is a preventative measure against most emergencies including fires, spilling liquids onto your desk, earthquakes, robberies, etc.

- Once you've backed up your files, delete the files that you won't use again. For example, I don't often look at the images on my iPhone again, especially if they are already posted on my social media sites.

- Utilize folders in your e-mail inbox. Delete e-mails that you haven't looked at in over a month.

"THE REDECORATOR"

Sometimes you just have to start over. This process/system takes a lot of time and can get expensive However, it is a method that works so if you have the vacation time, make sure to consider this.

You know "The Purge"? This is basically the same only at the same time, you're also painting walls and moving furniture around. My theory behind this method is this: when you move into a new home, most people want to keep their places clean and tidy. If you redecorate your home or even just move your furniture around, you can get the same type of feeling without actually buying a new house.

The same room with the same furniture can look completely different if you move stuff around and splash a new color of paint on the walls.

Chapter 4

An Argument for Minimal Living

Today's culture is all about spending money and owning the best and newest gadgets, isn't it? We're surrounded by advertisements that try their best to make you want to buy more products. They want to fill your homes with stuff that you don't necessarily need.

Believe it or not, you can actually find pure joy in owning less. This type of happiness comes with an intrinsic value that no product can give you. So let's briefly talk about what minimalism is.

It's not about getting rid of all of your material possessions. You don't have to live in a cave somewhere and shave your head. Minimalism is all about being happy with what you have, feeling comfortable in your space, and simplifying your lifestyle.

There are various stages and levels of minimalism too. Some people take it to the extreme while others take it lightly, making sure to implement the principles without compromising their new technological toys.

It is all about keeping and using what you truly need and love.

What are the benefits of minimal living?

You will be less stressed by your environment. You don't have to worry about cleaning as much. The fewer things you have in your home, the less you have to clean. You also don't have to worry about buying the newest and latest in home décor trends. You will find what you are looking faster.

You will have more freedom. If you're not tethered to material goods. You're doing something good for your environment by consuming less and making your carbon footprint smaller. You can spend your money on other things as well. Things that strengthen your core values. You won't need to compare yourself to others either. Being able to depend on yourself for happiness instead of material possessions and other people means that you will have the freedom to be happy.

Minimalism is visually appealing. A cluttered home is busy with chaos. If you live in a minimalist environment, you will find that your home is roomier and sleek.

You will have better things. If you spend less on buying a lot of things, you can spend more on what you really need or desire.

You will also find that you...

- **Can find work that you love**. When you don't have to worry about spending money on superfluous things, you can afford to look for jobs that you enjoy rather than just the jobs that pay more.

- **Are more productive**. When you spend less time cleaning and accumulating things, you can spend more time doing more important things.

- **Spend less**. Since you no longer have to buy superfluous things, you can save your money.

- **Make better decisions**. Focusing on your values ensures that your decisions will be based on the ideals that you value.

- **Make less work for other people**. The things that you do don't just affect you, they affect others as well. When you aren't consuming as much, making as much trash, buying things, or accumulating items, you are saving others from working as hard for your things.

- **Have more opportunity to rest**. Spending less time on cleaning means that you can spend more time with your favorite leisure activities like reading, working on your hobbies, or even napping. Some people consider that a hobby as well.

- **Have the ability to live in a smaller space**. You may realize once you've downsized a bit and have stopped accumulating possessions, that you have a ton of extra room in that big house of yours. You can save on your mortgage payments by downsizing to a smaller home.

- **Can manage your time for the things that matter the most to you**. Our time is precious. Being able to have time for the things that are high on our priority lists (family, friends, building relationships, professional improvement, personal improvement, etc.) builds character and can strengthen your value system.

So How Do You Do It?

Like I said before, embracing minimalist values doesn't mean that you have to get rid of all of your possessions. However, it does often mean that you get to downsize a bit. Decluttering is the first step. Here are some tips to help you declutter and help you focus on what is important to YOU during that whole process. In order to be thorough, let's go room by room:

Your Closet

- Go through your closet and your dresser and give away the things that you haven't worn in a year.

- Make sure to include the items that no longer fit. Sure, you were probably saving those skinny jeans for when you lose weight. Since you'll be getting rid of the jeans that don't fit in the future, you can trade in those bigger jeans for skinny pants once that time comes.

- Do you want to get rid of some of those designer clothes? Having prominent labels might feel good to you now but if you are focusing on different values, those labels might not mean much to you anymore. Try selling some of those designer clothes on Ebay or selling/trading them in to a consignment shop. If you don't want to go through the trouble of setting up an account or waiting for bids to come in, try a garage sale instead.

- Now that you've cleared a lot of those clothes out, pull everything else out. Take all of your hangers out and thin them out a little. What do you think is a reasonable amount of clothes to own? Does 30 sound reasonable? That would be approximately one item per day (not including the items in your dresser). Now pick out 30 things to add to hang up and give the rest away or throw them away if they no longer seem usable.

- Time to go through the rest of the stuff. Make sure to throw out:
  - o Socks that don't have a partner or have a hole
  - o Undergarments that you no longer wear for one reason or another
  - o Scarves that are frayed or damaged

- Cut back on your shoes. You should only have one or two pair of shoes in each of these categories:
  - o Dress shoes,
  - o Boots
  - o Sandals
  - o Hiking or snow boots
  - o Workout shoes
  - o Sports shoes (like cleats)

- Organize what you have left in a shoe organizer. Depending on your home, you may be able to have an "over the door" style organizer that you can hide in your closet or behind your bedroom door. There is also the "under the bed" type that you can hide under your bed, the bed in a spare room, or even under your couch.

- If you look at your finished wardrobe, you should only have between one and three loads of laundry to do if you were to clean your entire collection of clothes and undergarments.

Bedrooms

- Make sure that all of the surfaces are free of clutter. Clean lines are sleek and refreshing. In addition to that, they are also easier to clean (AKA dust).

- Make sure that you have a hamper. Don't ever put your dirty laundry on the ground. Not only is it messy, disturbing to the atmosphere, and a little smelly; it isn't good for your carpet. Bacteria can fester and grow in the most common of places after all.

- If you want to highlight a possession in your room (like your wedding photo, a stuffed animal, or your favorite piece of art), only choose up to three. If you try to highlight more, it will look cluttered and disorganized.

- Take a look at your collection of hobbies. If you haven't worked on one of your hobbies in at least three years, it's probably time to get rid of those particular items. Haven't knitted or crocheted in five years? You should get rid of that yarn collection then.

- Minimize the amount of furniture in your bedroom. Choose up to five to keep and sell the rest. The less you have in your bedroom, the bigger it looks and the roomier it feels. I suggest keeping a bed, two nightstands, and a dresser (or two if you and your partner have separate dressers). If you have a favorite chair that you don't want to get rid of, try incorporating it into a different room, and getting rid of something else in your home.

Bathroom

- If you haven't used a product in over a year (cosmetics, lotions, shampoos, soaps, etc.), get rid of it.

- Try to keep as few of each item as possible. For example, shampoo. Do you have five bottles of shampoo? Why? Dwindle it down. It doesn't meant that you have to throw it away. If they are all new (for example, if there was a sale and you wanted to stock up), use all of those bottles before you start buying new ones. I suggest keeping only one extra bottle lying around for emergencies. If you feel so inclined, I even suggest donating the rest of those bottles to a battered women's shelter, homeless shelter, or another needy cause.

- Lump together all of the items that you use for your daily hygiene routine. Try keeping

them all together in a basket or in one
drawer.

Kitchen

- Give away all of your duplicates. If you have
  extra timers, measuring cups or spoons, give
  them away. You don't need two electric
  mixers. If you can buy one item that can do
  the work of four, get rid of the other four!

- If you haven't used an appliance in over a
  year, it's probably time to give it away. For
  example, consider how often you have used
  your waffle maker, snow cone maker,
  popcorn machines, smoothie blender,
  personal sized blenders, etc.

- The same goes for your pots and pans. If you
  haven't used a particular pot or pan in over a
  year, it is probably time to give that up as
  well.

- We have a tendency of collecting coffee mugs
  at our house. Since I am a writer, everyone
  buys me a new coffee mug every year for my
  birthday or for the holidays. Yes, I love to
  drink coffee. No, I don't need five more
  coffee mugs. The thought is there (they were
  thinking of things that I enjoy) but I don't
  have much use for the extra mugs. If you
  have my problem, I suggest picking out your

ten favorite mugs and giving the rest away to a donation center. If you have unused coffee mugs, I even suggest possibly adding it to a coffee or tea basket for the holidays.

- Organize your fridge. Yes, it's probably long overdue anyway, right? Clean out your fridge and when you put everything back, make sure that all of the items are visible with the tall items in the back. I also suggest grouping everything together. BONUS TIP: dairy is the most temperature sensitive item in most refrigerators. Lump all of your dairy items together and put them in the back where it stays the coolest.

Household Tips

- The one item in, one item out rule can fit in almost every room of your house. Try your best to incorporate this rule whenever you go out to buy something. If you need a new shirt, make sure that you have one in mind to donate.

- Focus on being able to get rid of one item. Don't worry about the gigantic hall closet full of jackets that you absolutely love. Just focus on getting rid of one thing.

- Deal with messes right away. When you put something in the sink, don't just place it in the sink. Instead, make sure that you rinse it out and place it in the dishwasher.

- Break down large projects into smaller projects. Big projects can get overwhelming. If you need to clean out your garage, it can seem like a daunting task. Work at your own pace, turn up your favorite tunes, and focus on working on one box at a time. Remember that every box you go through and every box that ends up going out to a donation center or charity is an accomplishment. An accomplishment that you should be proud of.

- Find creative ways to display the things that are important to you. Remember that you don't have to frame everything and display everything on your coffee table. For example, having been a teacher in the past, I have a ton of artwork that I absolutely cherish. They started to add up after a while though and I felt horrible wanting to get rid of them. Instead, I scanned all of them in my computer and saved them as .jpegs. Then I uploaded them onto a virtual photo frame. Now they are all displayed on my wall and I don't have to worry about having a box full of drawings in my office.

- Remember to clean a little bit every day. Just because you don't have a lot of things, doesn't mean that the cat hair won't pile up on your couch, carpet, rug, and pants. Sure you'll spend less time cleaning overall but you shouldn't neglect your cleaning schedule all together. Dust is not forgiving. Dirty dishes don't disappear without a little help from you and your best friend, Mr. Dishwasher.

Chapter 5

Maintaining a Clean Lifestyle

Maintaining a clean house might seem like a big task. If you start with a clean slate (like "The Purge") it will be much easier. Maintaining a clean lifestyle takes discipline and dedication. However, it doesn't take as much dedication as you might think. Doing a few things a day can really help maintain that clean home and it doesn't have to take hours each day.

Schedule it out.

Developing a cleaning regimen can help with clutter as much as it can help with dust. I take fifteen minutes each day to focus on one cleaning/decluttering task. Monday is dusting. I dust a little here and there for five to fifteen minutes each Monday. I never exceed fifteen minutes though – because that's when it starts to seem like a chore instead of just a short activity.

A little bit goes a long way.

This is a lot easier for me since I have the option of working from home. But that doesn't mean that it's not "do-able" if you have to go to a workplace. Let's say you work a 9-5 job. When you get home at 5:30 and you want to lounge in the living room for a bit (detox from your hectic workday), pick up the room for five minutes before you sit down. If you want to sit and watch your favorite TV show after dinner, clean off the counters in the kitchen before you go into the living room.

Clean out your medicine cabinet.

This is an area that we often forget about. Go through everything and properly dispose of outdated medicines, those bandages that got wet, creams that you never use anymore, ointments that don't work, the bottles and tubes of things that are pretty much empty, etc.

While you're in there, go through your make-up as well. Did you know that make-up can grow bacteria if you don't use it for a long time? Yes, I'm sure that you loved that shade of lipstick that you used when you were in college but it's not going to do you any favors now.

Never leave a room empty-handed

I'm not sure where I heard this trick first but it is one that I've followed for a long time. No matter what room you are in, 99% of the time, there is something in that room that needs to be put away. For example, looking around my office right now, I know that I can put a bottle of Tylenol back in the medicine cabinet and put a roll of crackers back in the kitchen. If I were to get up right now, I would take those things with me and put them away, while on my way to my destination.

There is always something to clean up. If you do a little bit throughout the day, these small acts will help keep your home clean and clutter-free.

Have your family divvy up the duties.

Maybe one of your kids loves to put their toys in the right bins but the other likes to run the vacuum cleaner. Maybe one likes to help out in the backyard while the other likes to help you sort clothes. Everyone has a preferred chore depending on what they like to do.

I like being able to put things in the right place. My husband likes to wash dishes and do yard work. Because of that, we've come up with our own system – unique to us – on how to divvy up the duties in our home so that we can keep everything clean without running ourselves ragged. This also helps with cleaning up clutter since we both have our own systems set up for our personal belongings.

I, single-handedly, keep the container store in business.

Okay, okay, that might be a bit of an exaggeration. But I do love containers. You can get them cheap at places like dollar stores and thrift stores. You can get matching sets at big box stores. They comes in all different shapes and sizes. However, my husband tells me, that I often buy containers and don't have anywhere to use them. This may be true (but then I remind him that he does the same with his shoes and then he leaves me alone).

So what do I do with these extra containers? I look for places where a lot of tiny things accumulate: junk drawers, linen closets, bathrooms, the kitchen, the desks in the home office. I organize the small items into small containers. I like to use the small bins for our camping bins as well.

If you can get plastic totes in different colors, this can help you organize your attic, basement, and garage collections. I keep our holiday items in different colored bins: Christmas in red totes, Halloween in orange totes, Easter in lavender totes, etc. This helps me remember what's inside without having to look at through each one. Clear totes might seem handy in this situation but I prefer the privacy of solid colored totes. It makes the room look cleaner anyway.

Your labeler is your best friend.

For those containers that are the same color (perhaps the totes that contain all of your winter clothes), a labeler can help you keep them organized. There are a number of different techniques that you can use for this:

- Label each container with a number and name, then hand a map by the door with the location of each numbered box

- You can use your labeler to label binder tabs that you can keep in your kitchen to organize recipes, take out menus, or emergency numbers. Household binder and budget binders can help you organize the clutter in your home and your life.

- You can label your shelves in your pantry so that anyone that is putting away groceries or trying to find food can easily locate what they are looking for.

I also suggest getting uniform containers for your pantry and using the same font size for all your labels. Not only is it visually appealing, you will be able to read the labels easily without having to adjust your vision and thoughts to different (read: fancy) fonts.

Baskets. Oh my gosh, Baskets!

They are much cozier and have a bigger personality than sterile plastic containers. If you can utilize some baskets in your home as "catch all's" or as storage solutions, do so. Some ideas for basket use are:

- A lost and found for the living room. Assign each of the family members a basket so that as you clean, you can place all of their things in their own baskets (then, they can put their stuff away). When I was a teacher I called this bin the "unloved toy bin". The students had to earn those items back by doing good deeds. If the item was in the basket for a month, it got taken away permanently. Yeah, they hated me for a bit but they soon found a rhythm and we became a much friendlier classroom because of it.

- A catch all for the mud room. Small baskets placed in the mud room for things like keys and sunglasses.

- Guest towels. Yes, I am one of those people that like to display their guest rooms like hotel rooms. I have a basket that I place in there with clean towels and linens so that they can have fresh items for their stay.

- Toilet paper holders in the bathroom. Different bathrooms have different storage solutions. If you have the room to use a basket as a place to hold extra toilet paper, it can add some great personality to an otherwise sterile bathroom.

Downsize your wardrobe.

After doing a significant purge of our closets, we made a rule that states: for every item that you buy, you must be able to give one up. That doesn't necessarily mean that you should throw it away. You can donate it or give it to a friend instead. This has made a significant difference in helping us cut back on our closet clutter.

A picture says a thousand words, and can save you a ton of clutter.

I have an acquaintance that likes to give me presents. I love her to pieces and I appreciate the thoughtfulness but I find that I don't use those gifts often. In fact, sometimes I don't even use them at all. However, I do feel guilty giving them away. My solution? I take a picture of myself holding the item, then I donate it. The picture goes on a hard drive and I can feel free to donate the gift. After all, someone else might find use out of a zebra-print tank top.

One item a day.

If you want to minimize the items in your home but don't feel like parting with your items at all, do it little by little. Consider giving away one item a day. I like to keep a cardboard box in the garage: my donation box. The rule is: once an item goes in the box, it's not allowed to come back out. Put one item in the box a day. It could be something small (a keychain) or something with a bigger value attached (a sweatshirt from college that you no longer wear).

Do the 12-12-12 challenge.

The challenge is this: pick 12 items to throw away, 12 to donate, and 12 to put away. It might seem like a small, easy activity for the moment but think of it this way: you just organized 36 items in your home.

Enjoy your handiwork.

Once you've cleaned up an area, stop. Take a moment and really check out what you've done. I bet it looks fantastic, doesn't it? Enjoy that moment. Do you like how that looks? Good, good. This will be your new standard. Whenever you see some clutter starting to build up, clean it up! Don't let it ruin your space!

Board Game Solutions

Yes, we are gamers – but not necessarily video gamers (at least I'm not). We have a closet full of board games that we use on a regular basis. Game nights at our house is often bi-monthly if not weekly. To cut down on the board game clutter, we trade games with friends. This allows us to sample new games without having to go out and buy some.

The shelves in the game closet are lined with rubber coated wire pan racks. The board games can then stack vertically and won't fall over if you pull one out. Pretty handy, huh?

Jewelry Monster

My mom works at the jewelry counter at a major department store. This means that I get a lot of jewelry for my birthday and for the holidays. Oh, don't worry. I'm not complaining. However, this does put me in a unique predicament. I've never been one for jewelry boxes. They always seem a bit too ornate for my tastes, they take up a lot of room, and my jewelry gets stashed in drawers that I don't open regularly – which means that I forget that I have some of them.

Because of this, I – instead – use one of the top drawers of my dresser as a jewelry box. I placed stackable divided trays into the drawer so that I can find a pair of earrings easily. I also have a decorative corkboard behind the mirror. I attached the mirror to the corkboard with three hinges, then attached the corkboard to my door. I use tacks to hang up my necklaces. Now they are out of sight so that my spaces are clutter free – and I can see all of my necklaces when I go to grab one.

Laundry spaces

Laundry rooms are notorious for little trinkets. When we go through the pockets of our pants, shorts, shirts, and jackets, we find coins and other doo dads that we place on counters. After a while those things start to add up. Place some labeled jars in the laundry room to catch these things. You can label them by person (like those baskets in the living room) or my item ("Coins", "Buttons", etc.)

Chapter 6

Tips on De-cluttering Your Office

Tackling your Home Office

Your home office should be a place where you can relax and get some at-home maintenance done: sending e-mails, writing holiday cards, paying your bills, checking Facebook, reading... Enjoy your home office by making sure that you respect it as well. Clean up after yourself and declutter that room so that you can fully relish in it.

Taming that "Paper Monster"

Scan items that you want to keep but don't look at often enough. This will clear that stack of papers without making you feel guilty. Do the same with your kids' artwork. Hang up their drawings on the refrigerator for some time, then take it down, scan it into your computer, then you can feel free to file it in your, ahem, "circular bin".

Utilize that Pinterest board.

Do you have a Pinterest board full of images of your "perfect office space"? Instead of having an image of an entire office, try to find images of each piece of furniture in that room. How is it organized? What does it look like? Why do you want to mimic that in your office? Let's make an example of your desk. How do you want your desk to appear? Pick an image from Pinterest that you admire. Now what do you admire about that desk?

Now look at your desk. What part of your desk bothers you the most? Are there piles of paper on your desk? Dirty coffee mugs? Sticky notes covering your desktop? Start with the trash and clutter that bothers you the most. Toss the trash. Organize the clutter: file away papers, put those coffee mugs into the dishwasher, remove the post-its and determine where they need to go, etc.

Develop a filing system for your bills and accounts.
I find this to be one of the most important parts of a home office. Not only will this keep your home office organized, it will help your financial records as well. Win-win. I have two filing cabinets in my home. There is a two drawer filing cabinet in my home office and a four drawer filing cabinet in our storage space.

My two drawer filing cabinet holds my "active files". This includes a number of files that I have to look through at least once a year including:

- Appliance manuals, warranties and service

  contracts. I have since moved these into a

  binder however. I slip them into sheet

  protectors and keep them organized by room.

- Bank statements
- Bill payment receipts
- Bills that need to be paid. I check this about once a week and it's always empty but with more than one person handling the mail, you never know...
- Family health records
- Credit card info
- Benefits info
- Tax papers
- Insurance policies
- Encrypted password list
- Receipts for big purchase items that are still under warranty.

The four drawer filing cabinet in our storage space is our "long term storage file" which contains a number of documents that I have to keep on hand at the house, but I don't necessarily look at very often.

Clear your desk.

Clear your desk of all items. Now look at the pile of stuff that you just took off your desktop. Each of these items needs a home (not necessarily on your desk though). I like to keep things in drawers, cabinets, and on shelves. Keeping my desktop clear of everything except for my computer and planner is always my goal by the end of the day.

My organizational technique and system for my office supply will differ from yours depending on what items you use frequently. I keep a drawer for office supplies that I need on hand often. The rest go into a cabinet that I have nearby.

Organizing your Work Office

Keep in mind that a lot of the tips for your home office can be utilized in your work office as well.

Make a note of your trouble spots.

Take a picture of your office and make a note of the places that are especially cluttered. Keep that in mind when you are cleaning and putting things back into place. Are your electrical cords running in every which way? Do you have stacks of paper on your desk?

You might be asking, "Why take a picture"? Well, it can be hard to look at your workspace objectively when you're sitting right in front of it. You know where everything is. Items are easily within reach for you to grab when you need it. You've placed certain items in specific locations for a "reason". Try taking pictures from different perspectives to see if you notice things (like trouble spots) that you hadn't noticed before.

Add some shelves.

If you really have a lot of stuff that you need on hand, you can probably utilize some of that vertical wall space with shelving. If you can afford to put up cabinets, the doors should be able to hide some of the items so that your office still looks streamlined, clean, and clear.

Don't just look at office supply stores for storage solutions either. For example, putting pegboards in (or under!) your desk can help with hiding cables (hook them into place!).

Clear your palate.

Just like with decluttering your home, it is easier to maintain a clean environment if you fully clean it out first. Purge your office of things that you no longer need. Remember that your three categories should be "trash", "donate", and "put away".

Now add the stuff that you really need, little by little. I suggest that you put all of your office supplies in a box then go back to work. As you need an item, take it out of the box, use it, then find a home for it. If – after a week – you still find things in the box, chances are that you don't really need those things after all.

Reorganize your furniture.

I like a fresh beginning every now and then. It helps me stay focused, After a purge of your office supplies and clutter, consider reorganizing the furniture that you have in your office. Move your desk. Maybe even repaint the office. Put up some inspirational art (though don't go overboard with the décor). It'll be like starting a new job in a fresh new office that you'll want to keep clean.

Clean off your desk and clean your office every day before you leave for the day.

This is my biggest suggestion. Coming in to a clean office every morning will help you feel productive, refreshed, and ready to start your workday. It also helps keep the clutter down and aid you in maintaining that clean workspace.

Have a "go-bag" ready.

This might only work for a handful of you readers out there. For me, this has been a lifesaver. I have the ability to work anywhere. I work from my laptop and as long as I can hook up to Wi-Fi, I am ready to be productive! Because of that, I'm not always in my office.

I keep a "go-bag" handy for when I just want to change locations, if my internet is being wonky and I need to go somewhere else, or if I have to be at a meeting or an interview at a different location.

In my "go-bag" I keep a set of pens, highlighters, a notebook & folder with important information, and sticky notes. I also keep a flash drive in there so that I can back-up my work when I am on the go. All I have to do is slip my laptop in my bag and I'm ready with a portable office.

This cuts down on clutter because I don't need to search through my office supplies in a mad rush when I need to leave in a jiffy.

Chapter 7

Getting More Done At the Office

Setting up a plan to declutter your life in seven days doesn't just start and stop at home. For a full seven day week of decluttering, you're decluttering project will clash with your time that you're supposed to be at work. We briefly talked about how you can declutter your desk – literally. This time, let's talk about how you can declutter your mind when you are at work, so that you can get more done when you are at the office.

1. If you need to refocus at work, some visual cues can help you get right back on track.

2. If visual cues aren't doing the trick, why not have some audio cues instead? I personally use a mixture of both. I make sure that my work playlist is cued up and that my office is filled with visual images that are not distracting and help to motivate my work. I make sure to leave blank spaces so that my mind isn't too overwhelmed when I need flashes of clarity.

3. Getting rid of distractions is one of the few things that helps me no matter what situation I am in. Distractions can come in various different forms: loud noises, pets, coworkers, family, friends, visually annoying

objects, websites, etc. If you really need to get something done, make sure to turn your phone off, don't be anywhere near a TV, block all of your social media sites, and tell everyone that you aren't to be bothered for at least an hour. Declutter your work space of distractions.

4. Speaking of decluttering, cleaning off your desk can help you become a productivity master. Not only will a clean environment help you feel more productive, it will also help your brain stay on task because you won't be distracted when you have to work. Cleaning before you do work also means that you won't feel compelled to clean when you are supposed to be working.

5. If you work from home, one simple way to "declutter" is to simply close your door. Closing your office, garage, or shed door will help you create that boundary between work and home. Hang up a sign that says you are not to be disturbed. Sure, it might seem like you're just shoving all of those chores (that you are trying to ignore) underneath a rug but look at it this way: if you were out in an office or at a storefront, you wouldn't be home to do those chores anyway. Your work time should be spent at work, not doing chores around the house or watching streaming TV. Another way to help control your environment when you're at home is to

use a good pair of headphones to keep the "clutter" out of your ears.

6. Decluttering your team is important as well. If you have the luxury of being able to pick who you work with, make sure that you choose people who have personalities that mesh with yours. Sure, it is work and you should be able to work on a professional level with just about everyone, however, it is always easier to be more productive when you have people on your team who are insightful, encouraging, energetic, and hard-working.

7. You can declutter your mind by eating healthier snacks at work also. Things like high sugar and high carb foods give you a small energy boost when you need it but the crashes afterwards are a doozy. Instead, opt for healthier foods that naturally give you boosts of energy like blueberries, almonds, green tea, and other fruits, vegetables, and healthy proteins.

8. Decluttering your mind starts with what is in your hand. Set down your phone and slowly walk away from it. Put it on vibrate or turn the ringer off. If you are not fully engaged in the task at hand (because you are so busy wondering what the latest notification was), you won't be able to be productive at all. This is also a part of being present in your tasks.

9. You can help clean and declutter your mind by staying active as well. Do you have a lunch break, and two midday, fifteen minute breaks as well? Why not go for a stroll in the park or around the building? You can even go on a quick run. It will help naturally boost your energy level, make you feel better, and will help clear your mind.

10.   Grab some legos or building blocks and keep them in a small box on your desk. If you need a little creativity boost along with your productivity boost, you can inspire your mind by playing with these nostalgic toys. They can be a bit messy so grab a box that fits nicely with your décor, just to help keep your area clean.

Chapter 8

Organizing Your Life

Just like with organizing your office, bedroom, or pantry; organizing your life requires a process that will be specific to your interests and your needs. The process that works for a CEO for a company might or might not work for an artist, a writer, a clerk, a waitress, or an actor. Check out these tips. Try them out for size and see which ones work for you. Mix and match them, just make sure that you keep an open mind.

Write Down Ideas and Thoughts

Whatever you do, don't trust your ideas and important thoughts to your memory. You can easily lose your best ideas this way. Keep a notebook or small notepad in each room with a small pen or keep one in your pocket to catch random thoughts throughout the day. To cut down on the clutter in each room of your house, I suggest keeping it in a digital notebook: your smartphone, tablet, or even as a voice message or note. We all have a tough time when it comes to remembering things that we deem important throughout the day. How many times have you forgotten a task, to- do list item, or idea because you just couldn't recall it later? We may think that we can remember something "that important" but after being bombarded with information and stimuli all day, it can and will be hard to remember each detail.

Create Back-Ups of Everything On Your Computer

I'm not just talking about your documents either. Back-up all of your media as well. Back up everything on your computer but also all of your hardcopy media as well: photographs. Not only will it help you pack away some clutter, it will give you peace of mind knowing that your childhood photos will be safe on an external hard drive.
If you don't want to spend the time scanning them into your computer one- by- one, consider going to a local printing shop and ask if they will do it for you.

MiseEn Place Isn't Just for Cooking

When you are cooking, there is a phrase called "miseen place". It literally means "everything in its place" However, when you translate it as a phrase for culinary use, it means that you prep everything in advance: measure out your ingredients and set them on your table, then put the rest away. This eliminates a big mess while you cook. Having everything measured out means that you won't be stumbling over yourself. You won't be looking for ingredients, or spilling items while you are measuring them – when you are in a hurry.

This doesn't just work for cooking though. If you do this while you are prepping for other tasks, you will find that things have a tendency of flowing smoothly when you are ready to immerse yourself in the task at hand.

One great example is to start a ritual for work or for your down time. Having a bedtime ritual (for example) is important for kids as well as adults. Grab a glass of water to set on the nightstand. Brush your teeth and wash your face. Grab your book and make sure the lighting is right. Determine how long you will read for. Get comfortable. Put lotion on your hands. Then get to reading before bed.

You can do the same for work too. Have a ritual for getting ready to start work at the office. Clean your desk, set your planner out (digital or hardcopy), get the tools that you will need, turn the ringer off of your phone, have a cup of tea, coffee, or water handy, close your door, and start your work playlist.

When I work from home, it is even more important because the ritual helps me switch from home-mode to work- mode.

Check Your Home for Your Clutter Hotspots

A clutter hot spot is a place that acts like a magnet for clutter. It might be your dining room table or the counter next to the sink. It could be your nightstand or a few overflowing junk drawers. No matter where these places are, you have to make sure that you identify them and keep tabs on how messy they become. Keeping your clutter down will help your peace of mind and your outlook. A clean space helps your thoughts stay in order.

Keeping Your Bills Organized

One part of uncluttering your life is getting your bills in order. You can do this by getting an app that can help you manage your money. There are many that are available which can help you manage your bills, how much money is in your account, and how much money you've spent.
Each app has different bells and whistles depending on what you need. You can get graphs that show you how you spend your money. You can set financial goals for yourself. Some apps even have automatic bill pay options to make bill paying a snap. Most banks even offer services that may help you - like text notifications if your balance is getting low.

Create a Family Info Station In a Centralized Place

If you have a busy family, it is hard to keep up with activities and schedules. Soccer practice, recitals, games, field trips, projects, business trips, etc. Even scheduling dinner can be a hassle if everyone isn't on the same page. In this digital age, it is convenient and common for everyone to shard a digital calendar via Google or some other calendar app that family members can sync their devices into.

However, if your family doesn't each have a digital calendar or digital devices that can easily sync to a calendar, consider having an area in your home where you can all post schedule updates. In this area, put up a bulletin board and a wall calendar. Have all of the necessary tools at hand: notepads, pens, markers, sticky notes, etc.

If you want to get froggy, I suggest color coding everyone in your household so that you can easily see what everyone will be up to on any given day. Want to find out what time your significant other will be working on Wednesday? Look for his color pen or marker on the calendar.

Don't Leave Any Room Emptyhanded

I've said this once before and I'll repeat it again because it is just that important. There is always something to be put away – in every room in the house. Let's say you're sitting in the living room, watching TV, when you suddenly feel the urge to use the bathroom. If you're going through the kitchen in order to get to the bathroom, grab your empty bowl of popcorn or your empty glass and put that away, on your way to the little boys' or girls' room.

Getting in the habit of putting things away throughout the day and putting things away immediately will help you in life – and not just in the form of clutter control. This gets you in the habit of doing things as they arise (especially small, "insignificant" tasks) instead of putting them off to another time. Breaking the habit of procrastination is an important part of keeping an organized life.

Remember that, like small items and clutter, small tasks can also pile up fairly quickly.

Unsubscribe from Unread Digital and Hardcopy Magazines, Newsletters and Catalogues

We get a lot of mail in our email inboxes and our mailboxes. Most of that mail is either bills or junk mail. You can reduce the amount of junk mail that you get in both boxes by unsubscribing to the magazines and catalogues that you hardly ever read. You can find most of those things on websites anyway. This practice might also help you save money if you unsubscribe to catalogues where you often splurge your money.

Don't Forget About Your Kitchen

It's unpleasant to have to go through spoiled food from your fridge or to have to throw away. Make sure that you take inventory of your pantry on a regular basis – once a week or every other week, before you go grocery shopping. It's a good habit to go through everything in your desk drawers and junk drawers as well. This will help get rid of clutter and will help you save money on items that you didn't realize you already have.

Label all of your containers and baggies with the name of the product and the date it was opened. Don't forget to write down the expiration date as well. If you can measure out the size, I suggest that you label the quantity or size as well. Chalkboard stickers or paint are great options if you want to put labels on your plastic, dry good containers.

Create a Schedule for Everything

Some people might think that it is neurotic to schedule absolutely everything but it can aid in keeping everything running smoothly and to make sure that you don't forget to clean a room, run an errand, or check on something around the house. It might take some time to get used to this schedule but it will be worth it in the long run. Maintaining your possessions and relationships will take more time and a little bit of money. However, it will be cheaper than buying new items to replace them, if you don't take care of your things.

Create a cleaning schedule to help you remember to wash your windows every month, vacuum every week, clean up the backyard, and other chores around the house. This shouldn't just focus on the items around your home. Make sure that you get your car thoroughly checked on a regular basis as well. Get your oil changed regularly also.

Plan out appointments on the same calendar. Consider planning out your meals as well. It can help cut down on your grocery bill by having everything planned out. It can also save you time because you'll have everything plotted out.

Keep a White Board In Your Bedroom

Some people like to keep a white board in their kitchen and others like to keep a white board in the study. However, keeping one in the bedroom can help calm your nerves after a hard day and help you get ready for your day.

Put up a small to medium sized white board in your bedroom. You can put it behind your door or behind a small curtain so that you can hide it to help keep the bedroom mood.

Create two columns, one that says "To Do" and another one that says "Today". Under the "To Do" column, write things that you need to get done. Under the "Today" column, write down things that need to get done that day.

Having a white board to write down important tasks will help you sleep better and easier at night because you won't have these things rattling around in your head when you try to get some shut eye. In addition, having this available for you in the morning is a great way to help plan for your day.

Chapter 9

Creating a Bucket List

If you create a bucket list, it's like stating goals for the rest of your life. Of course, this list won't be complete when you first start it. I also suggest that when you cross something off, you replace it with something new. It is fulfilling to accomplish something big – like crossing everything off of your bucket list – but always having goals is a way that you can grow as a person.

Organizing Your Bucket List

Creating a bucket list can be a life changing experience – for the better. In order to utilize this tool to the fullest, you must organize it correctly. Think about the values that you care about the most. For example, I chose:

- Intelligence or Learning
- Create or Innovate
- Love
- Legacy
- Volunteering or Giving Back
- Exploration
-

These are the values that I want to continue to work on when I go through any type of personal development activity or challenge. I make sure that it fits at least one of these categories so that I can better myself in the ways that make me, well, me!

Now that you have your list of values (remember that your list can be as long or as short as you want), go through each value and start listing off activities that you would like to accomplish, which pertain to each category. For example:

- Learning New Things
    - Learn how to play the guitar
    - Learn how to speak and write in French

- Creation
    - Write a poem each week
    - Make Christmas presents for everyone one year

- Love
    - Get married
    - Adopt a rescue pet

- Legacy
    - Serve my grandchildren oatmeal raisin cookies
    - Become a world famous writer

- Giving Back
    - Volunteer at least 100 hours in one year
    - Read to kids at the local library

- Exploration
    - Travel to Central America and take a picture on the equator
    - Camp at every National Park in the US

These are just examples from my list. In fact, my list is actually over a hundred items long. *Why so much,* you might be asking. I intend on checking off at least five items each year – if not more! At that rate, I should complete my list fairly quickly, in relation to my age.

Another way to organize your bucket list is to do so by time limitations and time restraints. This might help motivate you if you fear that your list will just sit on your computer and not get done. You can organize your activities by various categories depending on when you want to finish them. For example:

- Bucket List By Season (Spring, Summer, Fall, Winter)
- 20's Bucket List
- 30's Bucket List
- 40's Bucket List
- School Bucket List
- Bucket List By Year

Adding New Items to Your Bucket List

Don't stop adding items to your bucket list. It can be as evergrowing as you want it to be. As soon as I cross something off of my list, I add something new to it. I like to change it up, also. I don't just work off of one category and then move to the next. I like to be well-rounded so I work on different categories at once. While I'm learning a new hobby, I also save money for a trip, and I work on poetry every week.

Taking Items Off of Your Bucket List

These things aren't set in stone. If you find that you changed your mind about something, take it off of your list. I have different versions of my list. Every five years or so, I go back and clean up the items that I have. Keeping the old version on an external hard drive allows me to look back and see just how much I've changed in the past decade or so.

Recording Your Accomplishments

I have a scrapbook in the style of the movie UP's "Our Adventure Book". It suits my personality but might not suit yours. You may want to use a chest or box to collect trinkets. You might not want to collect items; you may just want to frame your bucket list and cross them off as you complete them. You don't have to record your accomplishments if you don't want to.

I love being able to share fun stories with my friends and family. A photo album or scrapbook lets you keep mementos without adding clutter to your home. If you want to be even more clutter free, consider using one of those digital photo frames that will allow you to upload digital pictures.

In fact, why not post it publicly. Start a Bucket List blog for yourself or post your accomplishments on your social media pages. Have your friends and family hold you accountable by posting comments on your list and accomplishments. If you go the blog route, post on it regularly – at least twice a week. If you don't post an accomplishment or a description of one of the items on your list, post a blurb or an update about how you are doing.

Different Types of Bucket Lists

I also have a different bucket list for different areas of my life. I have one for just me. These are my own personal goals and values. I also have one for my relationship with my significant other. He and I talked about the things that were most important to us in our relationship:

- Trust
- Companionship
- Love
- Passion or Intimacy
- Adventure
- The Little Things

Using the same method that I used for my own personal bucket list, we began to add activities under each of the categories:

- Trust

  - ○ We each have a boys' or girls' night out each month.
  - ○ We have individual projects to ensure we keep our individuality in our relationship

- Companionship

  - ○ Spend time with each other during dinner whenever we can.
  - ○ Monthly Game Night with our friends, at our house.

- Gratitude

  - ○ We keep a "Gratitude Journal" that we write in at least three times a week. In this, we write down things that we appreciate about each other. "Thank you for cooking dinner when I worked late last night! I love you!"

- Passion

    o We have a date night once a week. It can be small and inexpensive as long as we are spending quality time together.

- Adventure

    o Second Honeymoon!
    o Romantic day trip every February for Valentine's Day. New place each year!

- "The Little Things"

    o Say "I love you" every day!
    o Leave love notes around the house.

This "Relationship Bucket List" makes sure that we don't take each other for granted. We get to talk with each other on a regular basis and we nurture our relationship instead of neglecting it. As you can see, we also take care of ourselves and our individuality and ourselves as well.

Make It Fun

Creating your bucket list shouldn't be a chore. This should be fun. You should want to set these goals for yourself. You can make it even more fun by making a date out of it. Get together with a group of friends or with your significant other and talk about what types of things are important to you.

Brainstorming with your loved ones can help you think of ideas that you wouldn't normally come up with. These people know you well and – because you are so close to them – they want the best for you.

It's important to create some ground rules though. No judgements should take place. Be open minded. Think big! Really big! If you want to become a movie star, write it down. You want to climb Mount Everest? Write it down! No one should judge anyone for their dreams and goals. Think of both big goals and small ones. Your bucket list should be a mixture of both. There is nothing more motivating than crossing something off of that list!

The words "impossible", "crazy", "silly", "feasible" or any words like those are off limits.

You can meet at a coffee shop or a local eatery but I suggest just sitting around your house with a bucket of popcorn and some movies that make you feel adventurous!

If you're a little shy about the items that you want to put onto your list, think about this:

- Teamwork: Checking off items with your friend or bucket list buddies is a wonderful feeling.

- Built-In Support Team: You're going to need some people to help you out in the form of moral support and sharing success stories.

- Loved Ones Can Help Hold You Accountable: When we are busy with responsibilities, personal priorities get pushed aside. Your happiness should be on the top of your list though. Share your list with your loved ones. They'll make sure that you balance your life between work and home. The more people you tell, the more you will accomplish.

- It is Interesting: Working on your bucket list will make your life more interesting. You'll have things to talk about. You'll be able to jump into different conversations about different things, instead of not being able to contribute to those convos. It is a conversation starter. It is a way to build connections and build relationships.

Partners in Crime

Having someone to do all of these fun activities with is a great way to spend quality time with your loved ones. While some items on your list could and should be done by yourself (it is important for you to do certain things on your own), it is more fun to do some activities as a group or with someone else. Grab a partner in crime. Share your bucket list items. Find items that you have in common, which you can do together.

Then, when looking at those activities, try to find material items that you might need in a "go- bag". My suggested items are:

- First aid kit,
- Some emergency cash (including some coins, a couple tens, and a bigger bill),
- A camera or extra batteries for your camera
- A water bottle
- A multi tool
- An extra pair of socks (and an extra set of clothes, if you can fit it in there)
- Some antibacterial hand sanitizer
- A towel
- A small bottle of sunscreen
- Lip Balm
- Bug spray
- Antibacterial hand/body wipes
- Kleenex

Starting Off Point

If you need some ideas to get you going, here are some items that might get those gears turning in your head:

- Slow dance in the rain
- Learn to sew

- Swim with sharks
- Learn how to ride a bike
- Complete a marathon or half-marathon
- Have a food fight
- Have a snowball fight with everyone in your neighborhood
- Kiss someone under a mistletoe
- Participate in a Humans VS Zombie game
- Have a Memory Jar and open it on New Year's Day

Don't forget that you don't have to wait to start crossing things off of your list. You can start trying to accomplish things today. Also, don't forget to keep it fun. If you add an item to your list, it should be something that you really want to do.

Combining Lists

You don't have to make your bucket list completely personal. You can also add a professional twist to it as well.

- Hit your sales goals
- Make a website for your business or your side business
- Complete your MBA
- Attend a conference
- Publish a book on your field of expertise

Your professional list should be just as important as your personal list too, depending on what your goals are for your future.

Chapter 10

Obstacles

There will be many different distractions that you will run into when you are trying to keep your home, work, and life organized. Here are some of the distractions that you should look out for.

Distraction

I can name at least five times a day where I am usually distracted by something other than the task at hand:

- When working from home, I find that I want to take care of the home rather than working from my home office.

- The 2 PM slump always has a tight grip on me during the middle part of my work day.

- Watching TV while cooking or eating dinner can be incredibly distracting.

- Morning breakfast and coffee time is usually meant to be a time where we can chat about our day but we are often too distracted by the tasks that are running through our heads.

- We spend time playing with our dog every morning before work and every night after we get back but often, I find that my mind wanders at this time, etc.

These are just five examples that come to mind – though they don't happen all the time. These distractions really limit our attention and hinder our performance. Instead of giving it our all, we are only giving it 50% of our energy.

Perfectionism

Being a perfectionist is one of the biggest setbacks to being productive. Why? Because when you are busy trying to perfect one thing, you are missing out on other tasks that you can be doing. Instead of striving to be perfect, why not do the best you can and leave it at that? You should be doing things because you enjoy them and because they need to be done, not because you need to have something done perfectly.

The Fear of Failing

Taking that first step into dangerous and scary, new territory can be frightening. When we do something new, some of us become overwhelmed with the fear that we may fail at this new task. However, people who are successful on a regular basis know that failing, making mistakes, taking missteps, and even taking the wrong route, isn't the end of the world. In fact, doing this is how you grow into a better person. Often, the most difficult lesson is the one that we learn from the most. How can you learn from something new if you won't try it first hand?

Consider writing as an example. Starting a project is always a frightening experience for me. What if I fall flat on my face? What if it isn't any good? What if no one wants to read it? Well, I won't go any further until I get that first draft done. Calling it a first draft helps cement the idea in my head that..., well, it's a first draft. There will be subsequent drafts that will be better as I learn from my mistakes.

Speaking Negatively of Yourself and Your Situation

When you tell yourself that you're not good enough or that you "can't do this", you are being defeating. This isn't the road to productivity and organization. It is the road to self- pity and loathing. You may even start to resent others who are thriving at the task that you are struggling with.

Instead of saying negative thought to yourself – about yourself – pay attention to what you are doing. Force yourself to continue with the project at a steady pace. Find a timer of some kind and set it for five minutes. In those five minutes, make sure that you are only focusing on the task at hand.

Don't think any negative thoughts. Don't switch projects. Don't get distracted. Just focus.

Also during this time, make sure that you are giving yourself some slack. If you are really struggling, acknowledge those feelings but make sure that you are moving forward. In fact, at times you can even use those feelings to help steer you in the right direction. What element are you struggling with? Can you find something or someone that can help clarify it for you? Can you read a manual? Can you find an answer online? Can you phone a friend?

You're "Too Tired" To Do Anything

Do you feel tired? Have you been sitting there for five hours at your desk? Is your butt numb? Are your eyelids droopy? While your body may actually be fatigued, don't believe your self- talk when you tell yourself that you're "too tired for this." It's not true.

Instead, stand up and do some stretches and breathing exercises. Get that blood flowing again. Instead of trudging along for the next three hours, stretch and breath for the next five minutes. Are you still fatigued? Take another five minutes to walk to the water cooler or break room and grab a cup of coffee or water. Then walk back to your desk. You're not too tired.

If you're still tired after that, it is probably because you're not taking care of yourself or because you don't really want to work on your task. Instead of moping and being distracted, focus on your task and why it needs to get done. Ask yourself these questions:

- What is it that I need to do?
- Why does this need to get done?
- Why do I want to do this? (And don't say that you don't want to do it. Find the reason why you want to do it – even if it is, "To get it done so I never have to see it again.")

What you are doing when you ask yourself these questions is refocusing and putting importance on the work.

Wanting To Swap Projects

As a writer, I can attest to this predicament as a major problem if it gets out of hand. I will be in the middle of one project, when I will suddenly be inspired to write something else. The worst thing I can do at that time is to drop what I'm doing to work on that new project. Think about it, if I continue to do this, I won't be able to finish anything!

Even if you are not a writer, I bet you can relate to this problem – even if it is something small. You may be in the middle of working on a report for work, when you have this overwhelming desire to check your email, social media, clean off your desk, plan out your entire workweek, or do some underwater basket weaving. Well, don't do it.

Respect your work and your creative outlets enough to finish the projects that you are on. As a writer, I keep a stack of blank notecards next to me. I use them to write down new ideas whenever they pop into my head. This allows me to put it out of my mind so that I can focus on my task at hand. This can work for your current situation as well.

If you're working on that report but you suddenly remember that you forgot to check your email that morning, don't stop and do it now. Just jot down a quick reminder to check it after you are done with your project or when you are getting ready to go on your break.

Chapter 11

The Hardcopy Planner

How many of you still have a hardcover planner? You know what I'm talking about. A little notebook that has a calendar in it. Most of us utilize at least one type of calendar – most of which are digital calendars.

The Advantages of a Hardcopy Planner

All successful individuals have a planner. It might be in the form of a digital calendar. It might be in the form of a personal assistant (who has a clipboard and a headset). It might even be a system which combines a hardcopy planner with a digital one – and a personal assistant. No matter what they use, they all agree that they need to plan out their goals, objectives, tasks, and lives in order to maintain at least a little bit of order and organization. First let's talk about the advantages of planning in general:

Planning helps you manage your objectives.

Planning will help you determine what your objectives are, and that's really the first step in being successful. It also aids in showing you're the purpose of each of the tasks and activities that you need to do. When it makes your objectives clear and specific, it will help guide your journey – whether it is for your personal life or your professional life. Think of it like a blueprint or a treasure map that will show you the path to success.

Planning will help you minimize the amount of surprises that you deal with along the way.

Surprises can be both good and bad. When it comes to setting goals and objectives, then following through with them – surprises often fall in the "bad" category. Both your professional and personal lives will be full of surprises and uncertainties and each of them will have a varying amount of risks involved. If you plan for objectives and goals, this should minimize the amount of uncertain variables that you will run into as you follow your path toward your goal.

When you plan, you are more likely to be able to coordinate with others.

Planning involves all sorts of goals. If you're planning for an objective that has to do with your job or career, chances are your goals will coincide with others' goals as well. Compare objectives and see where you can help each other achieve your wants and needs. When you coordinate with others, you'll also be aware of where everyone is expending their efforts and where your efforts are being duplicated.

Why have two people working on a report when it should only be a one- person job? Coordinating with others will also help you during evaluation time when you can all examine your own work performances. Where did you fall short? Where did you succeed? Where should you have been working harder? Which activities and tasks were unnecessary? Rectify your problem areas together, even if you are just aiming to improve your own work performance. When you work as a group, you can help each other see problems that you may have overlooked in the past.

Okay, so what's so great about hardcopy planners?

My organizational system for planning events and tasks involves both a hardcopy planner and a digital calendar which syncs to my phone, laptop, and tablet. That being said, I would be lost without my hardcopy planner.

- Recording your appointments by hand helps you remember them as well as provides you with a reminder when you look at your planner. The actual act of writing aids in memory after all.

- Planners allow you to record a number of things in one place, not just tasks: deadlines for bills and work, personal tasks, birthdays, reminders, etc.

- Gives you a broad look at your week and month without having to go through any trouble.

- You can record and schedule personal time: exercise, reading, planning, hobbies, etc.

- You can keep track of daily, weekly, monthly, and annual tasks and goals all in one place.

The Materials

I have used different styles of hardcopy planners in the past. Anywhere from cheap calendars that fit in my pocket to refillable leather bound binders. The bottom line when it comes to finding the right planner is that you need to find one that will meet your specific needs. My system requires that I have a hardcopy planner which lets me plan my daily activities, jot down notes in the margins, and lets me look at the month as a whole. I also like to have a lot of space to write. I may have small handwriting but I don't like being cramped for space when I'm jotting down my daily tasks.

What do you need to record in your planner? Will it be your only source of organization of this form or will it coincide with your digital calendar? What kinds of things will you need to record? Are you going to keep a daily task or to- do list? Will you need to write down notes? Do you need it to be portable or will it stay at your desk all day? Do you need it for your personal and professional life or just one? All of these things will determine what kind of hardcopy planner you will need. Okay, let's go over some of the important aspects of your different options:

Daily, Weekly, or Monthly?

There are three main types of planners. The first that I want to cover is the monthly planner. Use one of these if you don't need to jot down daily or weekly things. The boxes tend to be a little small but what you don't get in space, you save in..., well, space. These are the thinnest and sleekest of the three types of planners. They can fit nearly anywhere – even your pocket. They're the best option if you want to see big overviews of things: birthdays, anniversaries, holidays, deadlines, travel plans, billing deadlines, and a general view of how busy (or not) your month is.

Weekly planners are the most commonly used ones because they serve as a good middle ground between being somewhat thin (and not cumbersome) while offering you enough space to write down your tasks, needs, and thoughts. The planner that I am currently using is a weekly planner. In it, there are some reference sheets, plenty of places for notes, a yearly calendar in the front, a monthly calendar at the beginning of each month, and even places for reflection after each month.

Weekly planners are great if you want an overview of the week with enough details to let you know which days are busy and which ones aren't.

Daily planners are like diaries. They let you focus on what you need to do each day and usually have enough room for you do to a little reflection each day. The downside to this is that you can only see either one or two days at a time so you don't get an "at a distance" glance of your week or month. However, these are great for the really busy people who have a ton of things to do each and every day. You can record expenses, phone calls, meeting notes, and so much more.

What Size Do You Need?

This depends on a lot of different variables. Will you take it with you all the time? Will you leave it at home? If you're going to leave it on your desk at work or at home, it can be as big as you want. However, if you're going to carry it with you everywhere, consider how much space you have in your backpack, messenger bag, or any other type of bag that you might carry with you on a regular basis.

It's tempting to get the smallest planner possible when you have to carry it everywhere with you but you have to compromise between functional writing space and the size of the planner. Also look at your handwriting. Do you have small handwriting that is neat and can fit in small spaces or do you write large letters? Do you often draw pictures as well?

What Types of Weekly Planners Are There?

If you've never owned a planner before or if you're wanting to give it a chance and you don't really know what you need, I suggest grabbing a weekly planner. Like I said before, it's a great balance between writing space, overview, and the amount of space it takes up in a bag or on your desk.

There are two different styles of weekly planners. One has a horizontal weekly format which normally has three days on the first page and four days on the second page. This format makes it a little hard to detail your days by the hour but there is plenty of space for most tasks each day.

The other style is a vertical weekly format. Most of these have each day organized in a column by hour – but not necessarily. This format is great if you need to see how long each task or activity is. If you have a meeting that runs from one o clock in the afternoon to three, you can see that in the schedule, in a block format.

Binder or Bound?

There are perks to binders and bound- style planners. Each has their own pros and cons. In order to figure out which would be most beneficial for you, take a gander at these notes about each of the two styles.

The Perks of Binders and Bound Planners

Binder- Style Planners

Personal sized ring binders are an option that fits well in most bags. Most of us have seen one. You can refill them with sheets that you buy in store or that you print online. One great thing about these binders is that you can find a bunch of great templates for different types of sheets for these sized binders and you can also find a hole punch for these as well.

The binder style lets you put a lot in it because of the capacity to hold different things. You can find sheets and as well as pockets that you can add to your binder. It is easy to personalize that way. They also come in different colors which let you find one that suits your sense of style and personality as well.

There are also different types of closures, from Velcro to zipper, to buckle, and snap.

The A5 size is great because they allow you to write even more in them. I've always loved the personal size because they fit in any backpack, messenger bag, or purse but I always fall back to an A5 size because I need the space to jot everything down.

It is also easier to find templates for them since the page size is 5 ½ by 8 1/2 – which makes it a pretty standard sized paper. The downside to this is that they're a bit bulkier and won't fit in every bag.

Bound- Style Planners

I love bound- style planners because they keep me in line – figuratively and literally. Without the ability to add more pages (to an extent) bound planners are slim and light. The format is usually pleasant, sleek, and streamlined. They come in monthly, weekly, and daily pages. The daily pages make the planner a bit bulky but they are quite novel. They also come with different features, other content (like graphs, information, and handy data sheets), designs, and even motivational quotes.

The planner that I am currently using is a bound planner with the option to add just a couple of extra pages. It also has a large pocket built in the back page which is big enough for some loose sheets of paper, a couple sticky pads, a pen, and highlighter. It has an elastic strap as a closure, which can stretch big enough to close even if I fill the pocket full of stuff. That is one of the reasons why I don't like zipper enclosures. If you fill it too much, it won't close right.

Other Tools

There are plenty of other tools that you can use when you are organizing your thoughts, ideas, tasks, and activities in your planner.

Highlighters

Highlighters are great for color coding your planner. You can highlight different blocks of time or different tasks on your schedule or your to- do list.

Different Colored Pens or Pencils

Use different colored pens to write different types or categories of notes, times, lists, or tasks. You can also use different colors for different people if you're using the planner for a group.

Sticky Notes

Sticky notes are my favorite planner accessory. I use the small, rectangular sized sticky notes. I use them to block off different time frames in my horizontal format weekly planner. I can also use them to extend time at the end of the column at the end of each day. I also use them to change my schedule if I need to rearrange the events on my calendar. I use the bigger, regular sized sticky notes to create different lists in my notes section: grocery lists, additional to- do lists, a list of bills, activities, or for brainstorming ideas.

Make it Yours

You can add so many different things to your planner to make it fun to use. The more fun you are having, the more likely you are to use it often. Use stickers, color code everything, use markers, sticky notes, washi tape, colorful paperclips, buttons, and anything else that adds flair to your planner.

Pen Pack

In addition to you planner, you might want to consider a small bag or pack that has room for pens, sticky notes, a small notepad, paper clips, etc. You might not want to bring an extra pack with you. It depends on how often you are planning on using your planner.

At one point in time, my smartphone used to be the center of my life. I couldn't live without my smartphone. While that may still be a little true, I also keep valuable information in my planner and now the importance has shifted. My planner is the center of my organizational system. My professional career is written in the planner as are important contacts.

Plan Out The Important Things

Don't forget to plan out some time for yourself. It shouldn't be all chores, errands, tasks, and work obligations. Plan out some time for your hobbies each week. In addition, try to schedule out some time for these things on a regular basis:

- Meditation: At least once a day for at least fifteen minutes. Meditation doesn't have to be a super involved process but knowing the basics will help you have a successful meditation session. Look up some books on meditation at the library.

- Hobbies: At least once a week for an hour or a half an hour at the least. This could mean anything from painting to writing to building a boat in the garage.

- Date Night: When appropriate, remember to schedule some time to maintain your relationship with your significant other. Relationships don't grow and flourish when they are neglected. You have to nurture them in order for them to thrive – like plants or kids.

- Friend Time: Don't forget to schedule some time with your friends. Game night, movies, dinner out, hiking, etc. If you're a little short on funds, know that you don't have to spend a lot of money to see the people you love. Invite your loved ones over to your house for a little impromptu game night. Have it be a pot luck to help you save even more money on food. Have themes. Dress up. Each friendship is different so make sure that you group people that mesh and mix up the activities a little.

- Reading: Everyone should be reading a little bit every day to help improve and maintain your mind – fiction, nonfiction, self- help, etc. I like to have two books going at the same time, a book of fiction and a book of nonfiction.

Your time by yourself is important. This is when you get to work on personal improvement. It will also help introduce you to a life that is a little bit more simple. When you're not focused on what other people want or what other people want from you, you can focus more on what makes you feel good – which normally doesn't involve a lot of material things.

Alone time can also help you clear your mind. You can organize information in your mind when you are by yourself reflecting on your day. Don't turn on the TV or read on your tablet. Instead. Just soak in a bit of silence and clear your head. Meditate a little or sit back and think about your day. Your life can slow down for this time. This alone time can show you how to enjoy the silence or the little things again. Here's an activity to try: make yourself a cup of tea.

Instead of watching TV or reading something while the water is boiling, just stand near the kettle and wait for it to boil Feel the anticipation. Listen to the sound of the water. Feel the heat coming from the kettle. Be present in that moment. Do the same while your tea is steeping. Then when you drink the tea, enjoy the delicate flavors that blend together in your cup. Can you taste the differences in the various herbs? Can you pull out the lemon or the honey flavor? Savor the feeling of the warm cup in your hands.

You can learn a lot about yourself when you take some time alone. This is when you can focus on you: your likes, dislikes, what has changed about your personality over time, what you would like to try in the future, etc.

Planning some alone time can also help you become more independent. You know, you don't have to go out and enjoy the town with other people. You can enjoy the town by yourself as well. Go to your favorite café or bookstore. Watch a movie. Have dinner. There is so much that you can do on your own. Doing these things by yourself also puts the activity in a whole new perspective. You don't have to worry about the preferences of others. You can focus on what you want.

Most importantly, this is a time where you can focus on your own happiness. If we really take a moment and look within ourselves, it shouldn't take too much to make us happy. Maybe a favorite cup of tea makes you smile? Perhaps it is reading your favorite book? Maybe painting a picture or writing a poem? Different things may bring forth different emotions in us but happiness – that doesn't have to cost a lot of money or take a lot of time.

So take the time to go over your schedule at the beginning of every month. Look and see where you can put in a little alone time each week. It doesn't have to be the same time every week. This week it might be Saturday night after the kids go to bed. Next week it might be Monday morning before you go to the gym. Also look at moving everything up a half an hour so that you can spend the last half hour of your day in bed reading. This will do wonders for your physical and mental health.

Conclusion

I hope you enjoyed this book as much as I enjoyed writing it and it has helped you to take some of the necessary steps to declutter your home and organize your life.

Perhaps now you will see that de-cluttering your home and your life does not have to be as complicated or stressful as your first thought. So now, it is time to take action!